PRESERVED STEAM

Volume 2

Geoff Swaine

D1419684

Frost is on the ground as WD 2-8-0 No. 90733 puts on a fine display for the first service out of Keighley for a February Winter Steam Gala.

First published 2015

Amberley Publishing
The Hill, Stroud
Gloucestershire, GL5 4EP

www.amberley-books.com

Copyright © Geoff Swaine, 2015

The right of Geoff Swaine to be identified as the Author of this work has been asserted in accordance with the Copyrights, Designs and Patents Act 1988.

ISBN 978 1 4456 4946 7 (print)
ISBN 978 1 4456 4947 4 (ebook)

British Library Cataloguing in Publication Data.
A catalogue record for this book is available from the British Library.

Typesetting by Amberley Publishing.
Printed in the UK.

Contents

Above: *City of Truro* moves forward at Toddington on the Gloucestershire–Warwickshire Railway.

Below: *City of Truro* shows off her elaborate Edwardian-style livery and logo.

Introduction

For some of us, the love of 'all that is old' is overwhelming – the noises, smells, and sights which were part of our childhood. Fortunately, all this has been recreated for us at the preserved railways that have become part of our heritage. Now a feature of our leisure time, this industry has grown and grown so spontaneously that now it is unique to anything in the world.

On this small island, any distance can be travelled within a day, which makes the visiting of these sites readily available to most of us. For those of us who have the need to get among this industry from those great days, it is a great love. It takes us back to the days when coal was driving just about everything.

Whether the fascination is for the early days, or anything up until the 1960s when it all finished, a sight, sound and smell can be experienced.

A replica of Robert Stephenson's *Rocket*, with authentic coaches, is regularly out on show at different locations. Replica engines of *Locomotion No. 1*, the first steam-powered locomotive to carry passengers on a public line, and *Planet*, the world's first engine for passenger trains, are also out there to be studied and admired.

Rocket, of course, won the competition of the Rainhill Trials in 1829, and became the first engine to haul goods trains on George Stephenson's Liverpool & Manchester Railway, which opened in 1830.

Huge publicity surrounded the events at Rainhill in those far-off days of the past. Vast numbers of people flocked to the area hoping to see, or get a ride, on these new trains. Railway Mania was taking place. The spread of the railways throughout these islands reflects the business of private enterprise, where different companies competed against each other to provide services. This is unlike some foreign railways, where governments directed where railways should be situated. Those produced an ordered layout of routes with one main station per town.

Here in Britain everything was haphazard, often with routes being duplicated. Even the gauges varied, with Brunel deciding to introduce his broad-gauge system for the Great Western Railway. Chaos ensued where passengers had to change from trains of one gauge to another. Every early photo or engraving shows that, back then, passengers carried far more luggage than they do now. But things moved on through the ages. There was the elegance of the Edwardian period, the streamlined decade of the thirties, as well as the wartime and British Standard classes. Those marvellous volunteers and restorers have put it all there for us.

We know the reasons for the demise of the steam engine: all that manpower to run them, and not forgetting the daily preparation that was required before the engine could get to its train. People and business were switching to road transport in droves, exposing all those duplicate and unprofitable lines. It had to happen, and Beeching made sure it did. For us, the end was too quick and final – within a decade, all steam power on our railways had gone. It shook the enthusiasts to the hilt, so much so that when those early preservationist pioneers started to be successful in opening a few redundant stretches of line, a head of steam developed to lead to what we have today.

Britain did see a benefit from the over-production of railway lines that came about in the 1800s. In wartime, when one line was effected by bombing, there was usually an alternative route which could be used to keep the essential services moving.

For my generation, who grew up in the 1950s, the love of steam was there and exploited, but the intimate knowledge of different classes was limited by the geography of my existence. I regularly travelled between London and Somerset and, living in London, was one of those grubby schoolboys who hung around the end of Platform 10 (now 8) at Kings Cross Station. I also visited every station around the capital at one time or another. But one of the great things about today's preserved railways, and the media that surrounds it, is that it can be studied like a university degree. Everything is there to be learned and digested. So I say, to all you dear people, study and enjoy.

Early Engines at the Great Central Railway

Rocket, at full speed, heads northward along the double-tracked main line. The difference between first-class and third-class accommodation is well apparent.

Above: Replica *Rocket* stands at Loughborough station. Note the blast pipe which takes exhaust fumes from the cylinder valves to the base of the chimney. The intermittent blast causes a momentary vacuum, thus drawing the fire and producing a chuff.

Below: The original *Planet* was built by Robert Stephenson in 1830 for service on the Manchester to Liverpool line.

Above: Replica *Rocket* heads towards Quorn, proceeding backwards.

Below: Note the style of the early carriage. The carriage makers didn't know how to make a suitable vehicle, so they just placed stagecoach-style units onto a frame. A ride inside was definitely better than sitting in the truck!

Above: *Planet* replica from the Manchester Museum of Science has a rare outing to the Great Central Railway. The original *Planet* became the first dedicated passenger engine.

Below: At the same event is Furness No. 20, Britain's oldest working standard gauge engine, proudly wearing the Furness Indian Red livery. She was restored to working order in 1999 by the Furness Railway Trust, Barrow.

Victorian Times Broad Gauge

Broad gauge replica *Fire Fly* sits in the larger arch of the Didcot Transfer Shed. Goods from here would be transferred across the platform to be loaded on to a standard gauge train. The track allowed for both gauges before broad gauge was abolished in 1892 – the broad gauge being 7 feet (2114 mm) between the rails.

Above: On the broad gauge track is replica engine 2-2-2 *Fire Fly*. This engine is the only operational example of Brunel's broad gauge system currently available. It represents the original, which operated from 1840 to 1870. In the early days there would have been disc and crossbar signalling, which was to be superseded by the lower quadrant semaphore signals in the 1850s.

Below: The ex Frome Mineral Junction signal box controls the joint-gauge arrangement with a selection of signalling through the ages.

Early Engines

Above: The humble contractor's engine Class L No. 1210 *Sir Berkeley* performs some shunting duties at the Midland Railway Centre. The Manning Wardle of Leeds loco (built 1891) normally resides on the Worth Valley Railway. Note the very open cab.

Below: Ex Haydock Foundry engine *Bellerophon* in action at East Anglian Railway Museum. Built in 1874, it is thought to be the earliest surviving example of piston valves and outside motion in a steam locomotive.

Above: SE&CR P Class No. 753, in original lavish livery, glows in the early sunshine. This class came along twenty-five years after the Terriers and, being larger, took over some of their duties. Here at the Kent & East Sussex Railway, this engine was once owned by the Mill at Robertsbridge. At this location, the railway has hopes of connecting with the main line.

Below: Stroudley Terriers No. 3 *Bodiam* and sister engine 32678 *Knowle* buffer-up together at Tenterden.

GWR dock engine No. 1340 *Trojan*, built at Avonside in 1897 for use at Newport docks. These little 0-4-0 engines had to be quick to fire up, easy to get into reverse and able to operate on bad track with sharp curves. Usually operated by one man, they did not have a coal bunker, just a small amount of coal would be carried on the footplate. At preservation sites they generate considerable interest as secondary attractions.

Above: Two engines produced around the end of the nineteenth century. Built to serve the ever increasing suburbs of London. Ex LBSCR E4 0-6-0T tank engine (formerly named *Birch Grove*) was built in 1898. Here it is turned out in early Southern light-olive livery.

Below: Dugald Drummond M7 of the London & South Western Railway 0-4-4T was ex works in 1905, running as Southern Railway No. 53 (later to be British Railways No. 30053).

Late Victorian 4-4-0 Wheel Arrangements

Right: GWR *City of Truro*. Built in 1903 for fast express work, the classic engine moves forward at Toddington on the Gloucestershire Warwickshire Railway.

Below left: GWR No. 3440, in its fine Edwardian livery, stands beside the coaling area at Toddington.

Below right: The inside wheels with outer coupling rod crank definitely places this design back to broad gauge days.

Above: Heading for Medstead & Four Marks, the four-coupled pairing of *City of Truro* and *Earl of Berkeley* make a fine and rare sight.

Left: GWR Dukedog *Earl of Berkeley* is without nameplate at Sheffield Park.

Above: A study of *City of Truro* as she prepares to depart from Ropley on the Watercress Line. The double frames and inside wheels to the 4-4-0 arrangement shows where the design came from, but G. J. Churchward added the tapered boiler. The four-coupled driving wheels and small firebox may limit the engine's power, but there is no denying her turn of speed. Note the primitive springing below the nameplate.

Below: GWR Dukedog *Earl of Berkeley* is reunited with nameplate.

Above: The architecturally magnificent footbridge at Sheffield Park station on the Bluebell Railway. This is equalled by the pinnacle of rolling stock design; that of the Pullman Car set.

Below: London, Chatham & Dover Railway carriage No. 114 of 1889 forms part of the vintage train at Horstead Keynes. This four-wheeled Brake Third was rescued from its former life as a bungalow in 1997. Note the roof housings which once housed oil-gas lamps.

A visitor from Scotland at Wansford, on the Nene Valley Railway. Former LNER D49 4-4-0 No. 62712 *Morayshire*, in the early British Railways livery of lined-black, showing the lion and wheel emblem. Although it possesses three cylinders, the engine has a modest power classification, hence mainly being used for branch line work in East Anglia in its former life. Note the round top firebox and small boiler.

Above: No. 62712 *Morayshire* heads a goods train westerly at North Norfolk, where the line meets the A149 road.

Below: The engine glistens in the early March sunshine. This engine was built in 1928 by Gresley, but, by this time, the 4-4-0 wheel arrangement was largely a thing of the past. Though very popular in late Victorian times, it was G. J. Churchward of the GWR who preferred the extra adhesion of six-coupled sets.

Going to War

Robinson No. 63601 2-8-0 heads a service out of Loughborough station.

Above: 63601 2-8-0 O4/1 Class by Robinson, on home tracks at Loughborough of the Great Central Railway. This class was built for the Great Central between 1911 and 1920. The class was selected as the most suitable locomotive for the heavy freight trains required for war.

Below: A star of the *Railway Children* film. Class 25, 0-6-0 engine No. 957, typifies the workhorse engine of the period. Showing Lancashire & Yorkshire livery, she is not quite at home; Keighley not having been part of the L&YR.

Right: 43xx Class 2-6-0 No. 5322 was built in 1917. Given the ROD (Railway Operating Division) identity, she was shipped to France from new. Here, in authentic khaki, she trundles up to the Didcot coaling stage.

Below: In active service on the demonstration line, the loco is much more at peace than she would have been in 1917.

Above: The J15, built at Stratford in 1912 from a design conceived in the previous century. The engine carried numbers LNER 7564 and BR 65462. Now she waits to take the train out of Sheringham station.

Left: The integral four carriages of the Quad-Art set. Designed by Gresley for high capacity suburban work out of Kings Cross. This set at the North Norfolk Railway are the only examples remaining and are typical of the early high-capacity units of the period.

The Big Four

After the First World War, the railway authority had a quandary. What do they do now? The number of private companies who had their charges taken from them for the war effort ran well into three figures. The condition of the system eliminated the easy option of handing them back. The railways could be nationalised, but the preferred route was to bring everything together, with mergers, into four large private companies. There were a few exceptions, such as the Somerset & Dorset Railway.

The largest of the 'Big Four' companies created by the Railways Act of 1921, the London Midland & Scottish Railway (LMS), was formed on 1 January 1923. The major constituents for this were the London & North Western, who had the west coast route from London to Glasgow; the Midland Railway, which generally served the same areas but via the highly scenic Settle and Carlisle line; plus some large regional companies, including the Lancashire & Yorkshire Railway.

The Great Western Railway kept its infrastructure and was largely unchanged. The new London & North Eastern Railway took over the eastern side of the country. The Southern Railway incorporated four constituents in the south and south-west. The whole enterprise was known as the 'Grouping'.

Each company had a leading man, the Chief Mechanical Engineer, who had wide-ranging powers, especially in the design of their locomotives and rolling stock. These men became famous and their engines, to this day, still get a credit back to the originator. In the early days of the Big Four, the LMS had Hughes and Fowler. The LNER had Gresley. The GWR had Collett, who took over from the great G. J. Churchward, and the Southern had Urie.

In 1939, when war was declared, the chief mechanical engineers of the four railway companies were Sir Nigel Gresley of the LNER, William Stanier of the LMS, Collett of the GWR and Oliver Bulleid of the Southern. Bulleid had taken over from Maunsell in 1937. Gresley was to survive only until 1941, when Edward Thompson took over. Thompson, though, was only to last until 1946, when Peppercorn became the main man.

The preservationists of today are generally thorough in their preparation of engines to ensure the correct liveries are applied to their cares. With the stock we now have and the upgrading through the ages, such as rebuilding and superheating (with double chimneys), it has become much more difficult to show absolute true representation. Examples are shown overleaf.

Liveries of the Big Four
Railway Companies

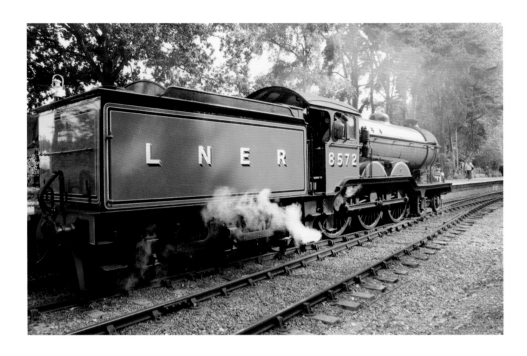

GNR-liveried N2 No. 1744
arrives at Weybourne on the
North Norfolk Railway to meet
ex-LNER engine N7, No. 69621.

N7 powers up the grade out of
Sheringham, passing the golf
course.

Section of the Gresley suburban
Quad-Art set.

Above: B12, 2-6-0, BR No. 61572, moves away to show us the very closely coupled six-set of driving wheels. A Gresley rebuild of a previous class with a larger boiler. They became Class B12/3, with No. 8572 being completed in 1928. Here it is at Holt station, the end of the line.

Below: On the way back to Sheringham, we get a full side view of the B12. Hugging the coast of North Norfolk, the engine approaches the final descent. Note the tiny tender.

Above: Two examples of mixed-traffic engines, first produced in the late 1920s, which became highly successful. LMS No. 5593 Jubilee Class *Leander* looking brilliant in crimson-lake livery.

Below: GWR Hall Class 4-6-0 No. 4965 *Rood Ashton Hall* is on the turntable at Tyseley; the engine regularly fronts main line tours from that base.

Above: The only surviving example of the Urie-designed N15 LSWR Class. The design was taken further by Maunsell for the Southern Railway and called *King Arthur*. It was used for express passenger work. No. 30777 *Sir Lamiel* is seen here in Brunswick-green livery outside the Loughborough works.

Below: Powering away from Loughborough station with a southbound service.

Above: The Southern Railway's claim was that this engine was the most powerful 4-6-0 in the country led to the Great Western Railway building the King Class. Four-cylindered No. 850 *Lord Nelson* heads a breakdown train into Ropley station.

Below: At Alton, which is the eastern end of the Mid-Hants Railway, the engine prepares to head the next train back.

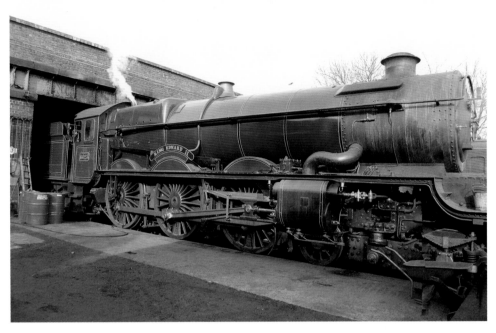

Above: 6023 *King Edward II*. The four-cylindered engine was badly damaged at Barry Scrapyard by having the rear driving wheels cut away. Fortunately, the preservationists got hold of it and completed a full restoration. Here at the Great Central Railway, the engine is resplendent in the short-lived livery of BR blue (1949–1951).

Below: The *King* reigns supreme in action on the preserved main line outside Loughborough.

Suburban & Branch Line

In exalted company. Stanier large tank engine 2-6-4T 3 cylinder No. 2500, which spent its life on the London, Tilbury and Southend line.

Fairburn 2-6-4T 1934 No. 42085.

The British Standard version No. 80151.

Above: Great action on the double-tracked section of the Great Central Railway, with two trains crossing at speed. 0-6-0T No. 47406 Jinty heads a southbound service, while BS Class 2 No. 78019 brings a service to the north.

Below: The Class 3 Jinty tank, built in 1926 at the Vulcan Foundry Ltd in Newcastle, brings her train back towards Loughborough.

Above: SR USA Class No. 65 (a veteran of Southampton Docks) approaches Tenterden station. The background shows the setting of the railway. This is the Kent Weald – the garden of England.

Below: In the same location, resident GWR pannier tank 16xx Class 0-6-0T No. 1638.

Above: The very efficient saddle-tank engines do not have the glamour of the mainstream engines, but provide an essential back-up to most of the smaller steam railways. Here is Hunslet Austerity 0-6-0ST Army No. WD192 *Waggoner*, on loan from the National Army Museum.

Below: An engine which made the crossing from the mainland – Beattie Well Tank No. 30585. One of three of a class that survived by working for seventy years on the Wadebridge–Wenford Bridge line in Cornwall.

Above: 0-4-4T '02' No. W24 *Calbourne* is back in operation at the Isle of Wight. This class was a favourite for performing shunting duties at Waterloo Station in the 1950s and 1960s. Here it is showing the 1950 livery, complete with the early BR lion and crest emblem.

Below: Steam is not all about engines on rails. The IoW Steam Railway also accommodates a rally for traction engines and steam rollers.

Above: SR USA Class No. 65. The very short wheelbase shows why it was ideal for working the sharp curves around the former Southampton Ocean Terminal.

Below: Climbing up the bank into Tenterden Town station, with a demonstration goods train, is LMS Jinty Tank Engine No. 47493. The engine normally resides at the Spa Valley Railway at Tunbridge Wells.

Streamliners

The classic lines of A4 *Bittern* are seen on the embankment heading towards Alresford.

Above: In Brunswick-green livery, A4 *Bittern* is seen here on the Watercress Line heading towards Ropley. Six engines in this class have been preserved, and this is one of four in Britain.

Below: The nameplate confirms that, originally, the class was named after wild water birds, before some of the LNER bigwigs thought it better that their names replaced them.

Above: No problem with the naming of this one. At North Yorkshire, Streamliner LNER A4 Pacific No. 60007 *Sir Nigel Gresley* crosses the road at Grosmont.

Below: At the Grosmont shed area, the A4 4-6-2 Pacific is serviced after finishing for the day. The plaque on the side of *Sir Nigel Gresley* shows that the engine holds the post-war steam speed record of 112 mph.

Above: In LMS crimson-lake livery No. 6233 *Duchess of Sutherland* waits at Swanwick Junction at the Midland Railway Centre to take out the next service. Designed by Sir William Stanier and built at Crewe Works in the summer of 1938, she was first allocated for working on the West Coast Main Line between London and Glasgow.

Below: No. 46229 *Duchess of Hamilton* exhibited at the National Railway Museum after being rebuilt in the classic streamlined form.

GWR Standards and Interchangeables

Above left: Mixed-traffic engine No. 9351 clears the tubes at Minehead before taking up her position at the head of the next service.

Above right: Lined out in Western Region express passenger livery is 5600 Class No. 6695 0-6-2T (built 1928), a Collett 'put together' of standard GW parts for use in the Welsh Valleys.

Left: The famous Southern Railway poster on show at Williton station.

Above: GWR Castle Class No. 5043 *Earl of Mount Edgcumbe* is on the turntable at Tyseley, where the engine regularly fronts main line tours from that base. The Castles had larger wheels than the Kings' 6 feet 8 inches, and could match them for speed. A good many people's all-time favourite engine. Built, of course, at Swindon in 1936.

Below: The original wheels of *King Edward II*, which were cut away after a derailment at the Barry scrapyard.

Above: A new-build engine in preservation, the mixed-traffic engine No. 9351 takes the lead from S&D Fowler No. 88. The front engine was controversially rebuilt by the West Somerset Railway from a donor tank engine – GWR Prairie No. 5193.

Below: A later class, coming in from 1938, was originally constructed from parts of the above Mogul Class. This example is GWR No. 7812 *Erlestoke Manor*, finishing the day backing out of Bridgnorth station on the Severn Valley Railway.

GWR Hall Class 4-6-0 No. 4936 *Kinlet Hall* runs onto the turntable at Minehead, while, in the image below, GWR Goods Engine 2-8-0 No. 3850 waits across the Didcot shed area. It is commonly thought that all Great Western engines look the same, and in this case the point is true. Both designs have benefited from G. J. Churchward's policy of interchangeability. Both have the same boiler – the Swindon No. 4.

Above: The familiar outline of GWR King Class No. 6024 *King Edward I* at Williton, the most powerful locomotive ever produced by the Great Western Railway.

Below: The new-build mixed-traffic engine 2-6-0 No. 9351 takes refuge in the sidings beside Minehead station. The similarities between this and the 2-8-0 engine behind are well apparent.

Above: Large Prairie No. 4160 (Prairie is the name for the 2-6-2 wheel arrangement). Part of No. 4160's working life was spent assisting heavy trains through the Severn Tunnel. The locomotive was rescued from Barry scrapyard in 1974. Its driving wheels are 5 feet, 8 inches in diameter.

Below: Small Prairie No. 5526 at the South Devon Railway (4-foot-eight-inch driving wheels). This wheel arrangement gave good balance for forward, or reverse, working.

Into War Again

Left: The Riddles-designed WD 2-10-0 90775 powers up the grade out of Sheringham at North Norfolk. Built in 1943, the loco was part of a batch built by North British Locomotive Co., of Glasgow, for war use. She ended up in Egypt.

Below: The Hunslet Company of Leeds made standard shunting and short-haul engines for war. Here, the Austerity tank is No. 23 *Holman F. Stephens*, named after the father of light railways. The engine is hauling passenger trains on the Kent & East Sussex Railway.

8F Goods loco No. 48305, built at Crewe in 1943, after which she was allocated to the LNER, where she carried the number 7652. Here seen approaching Loughborough on the Great Central Railway. This was the engine type which was selected by the War Department as the standard goods locomotive for war. In wartime, the standard livery was a very basic unlined matt black.

Above: After a long winter, the sun comes out for the Steam Gala in early March 2014. 2-8-0 WD 90733 is in action and revelling in the conditions. The loco, which is the only one of this wartime class to be saved, was rescued from Sweden, restored by the K&WVR, and is taking an afternoon service out from Keighley station.

Below: No. 90733, on the way back, moves tender first out of Ingrow.

Above: After twenty years out of service, the K&WVR's own 'Big Jim' American S160 No. 95820 was back in traffic at her adopted home. Here, the US war engine brings her train around Keighley curve to begin the climb to Oxenhope.

Below: The other star attraction of the 2014 Late Winter Gala. Three-cylinder No. 61994 K4 2-6-0 *The Great Marquess* bring trains away from Keighley. Both engines now appearing in BR lined-black livery, with the early lion and wheel logo.

A look at the Haworth preparation area from the road bridge. WD 90733 is coupled-up to the Midland 'workhorse' 4F 0-6-0 No. 43924. This pairing will shortly be moving off onto the running line to reverse to Keighley station to begin the activity of the day. In the background is S160 No. 5820, standing beside LNWR Coal Tank No. 1054. The public viewing area is on the right of the picture. This gala has given the chance to see two 2-8-0 engines that were produced for war. WD 90733 and S160 No. 5820.

Above: It is 8 a.m. at the Haworth shed where, this time, the locos can catch the early morning sunshine. Four engines are being prepared for the morning shifts of this Sunday morning of the Steam Gala. First away is to be WD 90733, ready for a day of heavy work pulling fully-loaded trains.

Below: In the foreground is the public viewing area, though there are not too many early-birds to be seen.

Above: Various pairings are an attraction at a K&WVR event. Here at the watering point is LNWR Coal Tank No. 1054, ahead of LMS workhorse 4F 0-6-0 No. 43924 (built 1920). The building in the background is the new Keighley College.

Below: 61994 K4 2-6-0 *The Great Marquess* waits for the resident War Department engine to finish. Note the opened-up signal box which is under restoration.

Above: With fires alight, S160 No. 5820 and LNWR Coal Tank No. 1054 are standing by to get in action at the gala running day.

Below: Architecture, once thought to be mundane but now considered a classic by any steam enthusiast. Seen on the ramp approach to Platform 4 of Keighley station.

After the War

Austerity continued through the post-war period because everything about the railways was so run-down. During the war, maintenance was limited to essential work only, thereby leaving a disastrous state of affairs when the railways were handed back to the four private companies.

Something had to be done, whereby the Big Four companies who had inherited the railways in 1922 were offered a way out. This time the government would nationalise the whole system, taking the railways into public ownership. The directors of the companies jumped at getting a government pay-off for something which was essentially a liability.

The date of nationalisation was 1 January 1948. The private companies had been regionalised, so the new system followed suit with Southern Region, Western Region, Eastern Region and Midland Region. There was also a North Eastern Region and a Scottish Region. Companies like the Great Western Railway, who had survived 'Grouping' in 1923, effectively came to an end.

However, the other nations of Europe, who had virtually all of their railway systems wiped out, were able to start again and go forward with electric and diesel traction.

Britain, of course, still had an intact system, albeit one on its knees. It required massive investment, but the country was effectively broke. The Americans had called in the lend-lease agreement, leaving a problem, so the railways were not the highest priority.

After experimenting with diesel power, it was found that the country couldn't afford to pay for foreign oil, so a decision was made to go forward with steam power for the railways. At least this power source was obtainable at home.

Without any plans for new classes of locomotives, the new regions were allowed to continue with building engine types that were on the books of the previous organisations. The Western Region built Castles, Halls, etc., the Midland Region built Black 5s, Jubilees and so on.

It was soon realised that some new planning was needed. The Rail Authority called in Robert Riddles, the man who had designed the War Department locos, to head a team to produce a whole range to be called British Standard Types.

Everything went ahead with these well-known classes until the British Railways Authority made the stark announcement, in 1955, that within a decade all steam would be eliminated from Britain's railways.

Above: After the war, the Bulleid Pacifics with their air-smoothed casing were hitting all the holiday posters on the Southern Railway. The Battle of Britain Class No. 34070 *Manston* is at the Swanage Railway preparation area. Behind her, on the small, 40-foot turntable, is BS large tank engine 2-6-4T No. 80104.

Below: A rebuild of the same class, No. 34059 *Sir Arthur Sinclair*, is at Sheffield Park on the Bluebell Railway. The West Country Class (see page 70) is identical to these and known as Light Pacifics with their 4-6-2 wheel arrangements, but the similar Merchant Navy Class are some 600 mm longer.

Above: Ivat Mogul No. 46443 (2-6-0 wheel arrangement) is serviced between runs at Bridgnorth. Viewed from the footbridge, the customers of the Severn Valley Railway get a fine view of the workshop area. Note the reduced bunker and tender half-cab which gave comfort and better vision to the crew when running in reverse.

Below: Of the same 2MT Class, No. 46521 is a Great Central engine based at Loughborough.

Above: Showing the great LMS livery, No. 6100 *Royal Scot* arrives at Blue Anchor station with a westbound service. The plaque below the nameplate tells us that the engine had a visit to the USA in 1933. This livery was allowed to continue after the war and into the nationalised period (after 1948).

Below: Looking a splendid sight between runs, 4-6-0 *Royal Scot* waits at Minehead.

Above: Running free in the country, LMS No. 6100 *Royal Scot* is in fine style on the section of line between Watchet and Washford.

Below: Newly restored in 2009, Stanier 4-6-0 No. 6100 *Royal Scot* runs into the platform at the end of the day at Minehead station. She shows off the splendid livery of LMS Crimson Lake, although the double-chimney tapered boiler and shaped smoke deflectors would generally represent an 'after war' style.

Above: View of Buckfastleigh station in South Devon, with *Small Prairie* 2-6-2 Tank No. 5526 getting ready to take out her train and head off to Totnes.

Below: The *Small Prairie* is well on her way, in a view across the River Dart. The train is on the approach to Staverton station.

Above: Collett-designed in 1928 from standard Swindon units, No. 6619 0-6-2T Class 5600 was designed for use with coal traffic in Wales.

Below: At the SVR, No. 7812 *Erlestoke Manor* has arrived at Bridgnorth with the Gresley teak-bodied rake of carriages. There are nine survivors of this class, which indicates that they are an ideal engine for this type of work.

Above: The classic view of Llangollen station. The train is halfway up the platform, owing to its formation. As the engine is in the middle of the set, it cannot get water from the usual location.

Below: A special watering point had to be installed halfway up the platform to suit this train. The express-passenger-green engine livery of the Western Region can be better appreciated from the platform. Though not altogether suited, the Western Region did apply this livery to a variety of engines in the late 1950s.

The driver of the auto-train is busily clanging the foot-operated gong, but the train must not lose momentum until it is right in the station. The train is on the severe gradient of the Berwyn bank. This set, with the loco in the middle, gives the auto-train the ability to carry more coaches.

Examples of two of the last pannier tanks to be produced for the Great Western, both by Hawksworth. *Above*: No. 9400 0-6-0T Class No. 9466 GWR (WR) Pannier Tank prepares to go into service at Loughborough.

Below: A type with outside motion, which pulled the empty sets of carriages in and out of London's Paddington station right through the 1950s. Here it is in action at the North Norfolk Railway.

Resident at the Mid-Hants Railway, West Country Pacific No. 34007 *Wadebridge* brings a westbound service into Ropley station, an example of the class that managed to escape being stripped of her casing. As a comparison, below is another West Country which looked like the above engine before having the troublesome casing removed. Rebuilt No. 34046 *Braunton* is seen in action near Minehead on the West Somerset Railway.

The GWR 'Halls' were ever-present right up until the end of steam on Britain's railways. Here, No. 4936 *Kinlet Hall* heads towards Watchet on the West Somerset Railway.

Above: Rebuilt 4-6-2 West Country Class, No. 34036 *Braunton* is piloted by Black 5 4-6-0 No. 45231 *The Sherwood Forester*. The train slows the pace on the approach to Minehead station.

Below: The fine pairing stay together for a trip in the other direction. Now having left Williton, they turn southward towards Bishops Lydeard. Both engines represent the post-nationalisation period, with *Braunton* representing the Southern Region and the Black 5 representing the Midland Region.

BR Standards

BR Standard Class 4-6-2 No. 71000 *Duke of Gloucester* winds down at the shed area of Bridgnorth station on the Severn Valley Railway. As a class of one locomotive, she was commissioned to replace No. 46202 *Princess Anne*, which was lost in the 1952 crash at Harrow & Wealdstone.

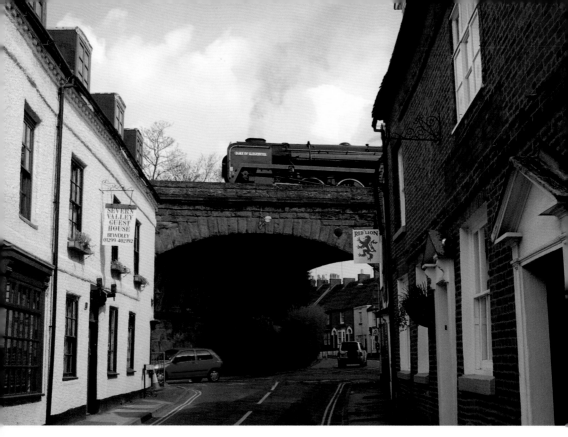

Above: 71000 *Duke of Gloucester* crosses the B4190 road at Bewdley.

Below: Some of the double-sausage totems that didn't slip into the hands of private owners are at the Kidderminster station museum.

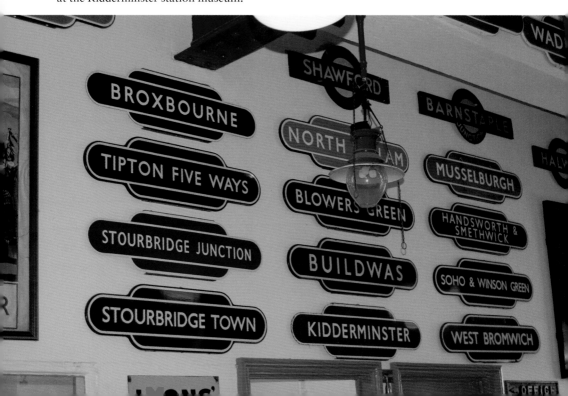

Running free on the Great Central main line with a scheduled service is 2-6-0 Standard Class 2 No. 78019. It is considered to be the perfect engine for a preserved railway when the heaviest loads are not expected. Below is the side view of the engine as it goes out of service at Loughborough. Note the cold water feed position halfway between the chimney and dome.

Above: On the North Norfolk Railway, there was such an intensive service for the March 2015 Gala that BR Class 4 2-6-0 No. 76084 took one service out with the DMU set. On the embankment before crossing the A149 road, the train heads for Weybourne.

Below: On the way back, and with the sea in the distance, the engine approaches the gradient down into Sheringham station.

Above: No. 73050 *City of Peterborough* picks up steam as she prepares to take the next service out of Wansford station on the Nene Valley Railway. Note the Continental coaching stock on the adjoining line.

Below: The BR Standard 5 4-6-0, built in 1954, sits in the sunshine at the NVR shed area. No. 73050 is now named *City of Peterborough*, becoming the flagship of the railway.

Above: BR Standard Class 5MT No. 73129 was built at Derby Loco Works in 1956. The class was designed to supersede the Black 5s.

Below: Without a headcode, Riddles Standard 5 waits at Butterley station at the Midland Railway Centre with a double-headed service. This engine was part of the last batch of thirty 5MTs to be built, they were fitted with Caprotti valve gear (rotary rather than sliding valve connectors) and No. 73129 is the only survivor.

Above: Visiting from the Llangollen Railway is British Standard 2-6-4T Class 4 No. 80072 large tank engine, seen here disappearing below the newly completed overall roof at Pickering station.

Below: British Standard 9F 2-10-0 No. 92214 carrying the short-lived name *Cock o' the North*. Pickering station can be seen in the background, proudly displaying the new roof.

Above: No. 92203 *Black Prince* 2-10-0 waits with a train at north Norfolk's Weybourne station while BR Class 4 2-6-0 No. 76084 comes through with an eastbound service.

Below: Again *Black Prince* waits, but this time at the Gloucestershire Warwickshire Railway. Winchcombe's starter signal holds her for Western Region tank No. 5619 to bring in a southbound train.

Above: British Standard Class 9F No. 92214 pulls the loose-coupled goods train eastwards, along cob beside Butterley reservoir, from the little hamlet of Hammersmith.

Below: At the same Midland Railway Centre, No. 92219 has (so far) lost out in the restoration stakes. She has just been a donor engine to No. 92214 for spares. Both had been sold for scrap to Woodham Bros, of Barry, after withdrawal by British Railways in 1965.

Two engines with a David Shepherd connection. No. 92203 *Black Prince* 2-10-0 brings a northbound train into Toddington station on the Gloucestershire Warwickshire Railway. Note the wildlife foundation sign on the front. Below, British Standard Class 4 No. 75029 waits for the green light at Grosmont depot on the North York Moors Railway. This engine was the second to be purchased by artist David Shepherd direct from British Railways. He gave it the name *The Green Knight*.

Preservation

A view of Corfe Castle.

The station sign at Corfe Castle.

Above: Getting the all-clear from the starter signal, the train, headed by No. 53, gets underway heading eastwards towards Swanage.

Below: The classic scene of the railway. LSWR 0-4-4 Class M7 No. 53 (BR 30053) approaches Corfe Castle station from Norden. This section of line was reopened in 1995.

Above: The primroses are in bloom as the train passes right under Corfe Castle. Dugaid Drummond M7 L&SWR 0-4-4T, running as Southern Railway No. 53 (later to be British Railways No. 30053).

Below: The engine moves off from Corfe Castle station towards Swanage. The engine was sold to American owners in 1967, only to be returned to England in 1987. One other of the class has survived and is now part of the National Collection.

Above: View from Corfe Castle as the service to Norden has just left the village station. An opposite view to that of the station platform.

Below: Having left Corfe Castle, the train moves along on towards Norden. The classic Southern dark olive-green livery of the carriages was sadly phased out from 1967.

Above: LMS Ivatt mogul (2-6-2 wheel arrangement) 4MT No. 46443 crosses the flying span of the Victoria Bridge with a northbound service.

Below: A closer view of the LMS Stanier No. 42968 from the west side of the shed area at Bridgnorth. Latecomers can enjoy some fine close views of the stock, seen here soaking up the evening sunshine.

No. 5239 2-8-0T *Goliath* engine buffers up to the 'Devon Belle' observation coach at Kingswear for the return trip to Paignton. Note the fully lined-out livery, the engine now has star billing, quite unlike anything from her former life in those Welsh coal fields. Travellers on the steam railway can transfer onto a river cruise to be carried by a variety of craft, including the paddle steamer *Kingswear Castle*.

On the Main Line

Above: K1 2-6-0 No. 62005 takes her train, 'The Jacobite', along the West Highland Line. The train crosses the curving Glenfinnan Viaduct, built in 1898 with twenty-one arches by 'Concrete Bob' McAlpine, founder of the famous construction company.

Below: Un-rebuilt Bulleid Battle of Britain Pacific 4-6-2 No. 34067 *Tangmere* hurries past *Olympia* on the West London Line, heading a 'Golden Arrow Statesman' Pullman to Canterbury.

Above: Celebrating the 150th anniversary of the opening of the Hammersmith and City extension of the Metropolitan Railway 1864. We see Metropolitan electric No. 12 *Sarah Siddons* having just arrived at Hammersmith station.

Below: Getting ready for the eastbound run, Metropolitan Locomotive 0-4-4T No. 1 is at the head with the milk-van just behind. The carriages are the restored 'Chesham' set from the Bluebell Railway dating from 1896–1900.

Above: A view of the classic curved train shed at Bristol Temple Meads, as the former London Midland & Scottish engine LMS 5MT 4-6-0 No. 45407 *The Lancashire Fusilier* backs in to take a steam special into Devon and back.

Below: The Torbay Express was one of the great named trains which ran daily from London to the West Country. The final destination being Kingswear, which is where we see the train arriving. Headed by Rebuilt Bulleid Pacific No. 34046 *Braunton*.

Above: With a new power unit built at Didcot, Steam Railmotor No. 93 waits at Southall before getting underway with a keen set of passengers. A bunker on the train can hold about 3 cwt of coal. The Railmotor has 'come home' to Southall, where it began its working life in 1908.

Below: No. 35028 *Clan Line* had the good fortune to be sold into private ownership straight from British Railways in 1967. Here she takes out a lunchtime special from Victoria. The train makes the Thames crossing as seen from Chelsea Bridge.

The signal gantry rescued from Scarborough has found a new home at Grosmont in North Yorkshire. From this point, the Whitby extension begins. Black 5 No. 45428 *Eric Treacy* is passing below the impressive gantry.

Schedule of Lines (Standard Gauge)

Alderney Railway
Alderney, C.I.
www.alderneyrailway.com
Tel: 01455 634373

Avon Valley Railway
Bitton Station, Near Bristol,
BS30 6HD
www.avonvalleyrailway.org.uk
Tel: 01457 484950

Barrow Hill Roundhouse
Chesterfield, Derbyshire,
S43 2PR
www.barrowhill.org.uk
Tel: 01246 472450

Barry Tourist Railway
www.barrytouristrailway.co.uk
Tel: 01446 748816

Battlefield Line Railway
Shackerstone Station,
CV13 6NW
www.battlefield-line-railway.
co.uk
Tel: 01827 880754

Bluebell Railway
Sheffield Park Station,
TN22 3QL
Horsted Keynes Station,
RH17 7BB
www.bluebell-railway.co.uk
Tel: 01825 720800

Bodmin & Wenford Railway
Bodmin General Station,
PL31 1AQ
www.bodminrailway.co.uk
Tel: 01208 73666

Bo'Ness & Kinneil Railway
Bo'ness Station, EH51 9AQ
www.bkrailway.co.uk
Tel: 01506 825855

Bowes Railway Centre
Gateshead, NE9 7QJ

www.newcastlegateshead.com
Tel: 01914 161847

Bressingham Steam Museum
Near Diss, Norfolk, IP22 2AA
www.bressingham.co.uk
Tel: 01379 686900

Bristol Harbour Railway
Princes Wharf, BS1 4RN
www.bristolharbourrailway.
co.uk
Tel: 01173 526600

Buckingham Railway Centre
Quainton Road Station,
HP22 4BY
www.bucksrailcentre.org.uk
Tel: 01296 655720

Caledonian Railway
Brechin Station, DD97AF
www.caledonian-railway.com
Tel: 01356 622992

Chasewater Railway
Brownhills West, WS8 7NL
www.chasewaterrailway.co.uk
Tel: 01543 452623

Chinnor & Princes Risborough
Railway
Chinnor Station, OX39 4ER
www.chinnorrailway.co.uk
Talking Timetable: 01844
353535

Cholsey & Wallingford Railway
Wallingford, OX10 9GQ
www.cholsey-wallingford-
railway.com
Tel: 01491 835067

Churnet Valley Railway
Kingsley & Froghall Station,
ST10 2HA
www.churnet-valley-railway.
org.uk
Tel: 01538 750755

Colne Valley Railway
Castle Hedingham,
CO9 3DZ
www.colnevalleyrailway.co.uk
Tel: 01787 461174

Darlington Railway Museum
Station Rd, Darlington,
DL3 6ST
www.darlington.gov.uk
Tel: 01325 460532

Dartmoor Railway
Oakhampton, EX20 1EJ
www.dartmoorrailway.com
Tel: 01837 55164

Dartmouth Steam Railway &
River Boat Company
Paignton, TQ4 6AF
www.dartmouthrailriver.co.uk
Tel: 01803 555872

Dean Forest Railway
Lydney, GL15 4ET
www.deanforestrailway.co.uk
Tel: 01594 845840

Derwent Valley Light Railway
Murton Park, York,
YO19 5UF
www.dvlr.org.uk
Tel: 01904 489966

Didcot Railway Centre
Didcot, OX11 7NJ
www.didcotrailwaycentre.
org.uk
Tel: 01235 817200

Downpatrick & Co. Down
Railway
Downpatrick Station. N.I.,
BT30 6LZ
www.downrail.co.uk
Tel: 02844 612233

East Anglian Railway Museum
Chappel, Near Colchester,

CO6 2DS
www.earm.co.uk
Tel: 01206 242524

East Kent Railway
Shepherdswell, CT15 7PD
www.eastkentrailway.co.uk
Tel: 01304 832042

East Somerset Railway
Cranmore Station, BA4 4QP
www.eastsomersetrailway.
co.uk
Tel: 01749 880417

East Lancashire Railway
Bury Bolton Street Station,
BL9 0EY
Rawtenstall Station,
BB4 6DD
Ramsbottom Station, BL0 9AL
www.eastlancsrailway.org.uk
Tel: 01617 647790

Ecclesbourne Valley Railway
Wicksworth, DE4 4FB
www.e-v-r.com
Tel: 01629 823076

Elsecar Heritage Railway
Elscar Heritage Centre,
S74 8HJ
www.elsecarrailway.co.uk
Tel: 01226 740203

Embsay & Bolton Abbey
Steam Railway
Bolton Abbey Station, Skipton.
BD23 6AF.
www.
embsayboltonabbeyrailway.
org.uk
Tel: 01756 710614
Talking Timetable: 01756
795189

Epping–Ongar Railway
Ongar Town, CM5 9AB
www.eorailway.co.uk
Tel: 01277 365200

Foxfield Steam Railway
Blythe Bridge, ST11 9BG
www.foxfieldrailway.co.uk
Tel: 01782 396210

Gloucestershire Warwickshire
Railway
Toddington Station, GL54 5DT
Winchcombe Station,
GL54 5LB
www.gwsr.com
Tel: 01242 621405

Great Central Railway
Loughborough Central Station,
LE11 1RW
Quorn & Woodhouse,
LE12 8AW
Leicester North, LE4 3BR
www.gcrailway.co.uk
Tel: 01509 632323

Gt Central–Nottingham
Ruddington, NG11 6JS
www.gcrn.co.uk
Tel: 0115 9405705

Gwili Railway
Carmarthen, SA33 6HT
www.gwili-railway.co.uk
Tel: 01267 230666

GWR (Steam Museum)
Swindon, SN2 2EY
www.steam-museum.org.uk
Tel: 01793 466646

Isle of Wight Steam Railway
Havenstreet, PO33 4DS
www.iwsteamrailway.co.uk
Tel: 01983 882204

Keighly & Worth Valley
Railway
Haworth Station, BD22 8NJ
Keighley Station, BD21 4HP
www.kwvr.co.uk
Tel: 01535 645214

Kent & East Sussex Railway
Tenterden Station, TN30 6HE
www.kesr.org.uk
Tel: 01580 765155
Talking Timetable: 01580
762943

Lakeside & Haverthwaite
Railway
Haverthwaite Station, LA12
8AL

www.lakesiderailway.co.uk
Tel: 01539 531594

Lavender Line
Isfield Station, TN22 5XB
www.lavender-line.co.uk
Tel: 01825 750515

Lincolnshire Wolds Railway
Ludborough, DN36 5SH
www.lincolnshirewoldsrailway.
co.uk
Tel: 01507 363881

Lllangollen Railway
Llangollen Station, LL20 8SN
www.llangollen-railway.co.uk
Tel: 01978 860979

Mangapps Farm Railway
Museum
Burnham-on-Crouch,
CM0 8QG
www.mangapps.co.uk
Tel: 01621 784898

Middleton Railway
Hunslet, LS10 2JQ
www.middletonrailway.org.uk
Tel: 0845 680 1758

Mid-Norfolk Railway
Dereham Station, NR19 1DF
www.mnr.org.uk
Tel: 01362 851723

Mid-Hants Railways
(Watercress Line)
Railway Station Alresford,
SO24 9JG
Ropley Station, SO24 0BL
www.watercressline.co.uk
Tel: 01962 733810

Midland Railway Centre
Butterley Station, DE5 3QZ
Swanwick Junction
www.midlandrailwaycentre.
co.uk
Tel: 01773 570140

Mid-Suffolk Light Railway
Wetheringsett, IP14 5PW
www.mslr.org.uk
Tel: 01449 766899

National Railway Museum
Leeman Road, York, YO26 4XL
www.nrm.org.uk
Tel: 08448 153139

Nene Valley Railway
Wansford Station, PE8 6LR
www.nvr.org.uk
Tel: 01780 784444

Northampton & Lamport
Railway
Pitsford & Brampton Station,
NN6 8BA
www.nlr.org.uk
Tel: 01604 820327

Northamptonshire Ironside
Railway Trust
Northampton, NN4 9UW
www.nirt.co.uk
Tel: 01604 702031

North Norfolk Railway
Sheringham Station, NR26
8RA
Holt Station, NR25 6AJ
www.nnrailway.co.uk
Tel; 01263 820800

North Tyneside Steam Railway
(Stephenson Railway Museum)
North Shields, NE29 8DX
www.twmuseums.org.uk

North York Moors Railway
Pickering, YO18 7AJ
Goathland, YO22 5NF
Grosmont, YO22 5QE
www.nymr.co.uk
Tel: 01751 472508

Pallot Steam, Motor & General
Museum
Jersey, C.I.

www.pallotmuseum.co.uk
Tel: 01534 865307

Peak Rail
Matlock, DE4 3NA
www.peakrail.co.uk
Tel: 01629 580381

Plym Valley Railway
Plympton, PL7 4NW
www.plymrail.co.uk

Pontypool & Blaenavon
Railway
Blaenavon, NP4 9ND
www.pontypool-and-
blaenavon.co.uk
Tel: 01495 792263

Railway Preservation Society
of Ireland
www.steamtrainsireland.com

Rutland Railway Museum
Cottesmore, LE15 7BX
www.rutnet.co.uk
Tel: 01572 813203

Severn Valley Railway
Bridgnorth, WV16 5DT
Bewdley, DY12 1BG
Kidderminster, DY10 1QX
www.svr.co.uk
Tel: 01299 403816

South Devon Railway
Buckfastleigh, TQ11 0DZ
www.southdevonrailway.
co.uk
Tel: 08433571420

Southall Railway Centre
Southall, UB2 4SE
www.gwrpg.co.uk
Tel: 0208 574 1529

Spa Valley Railways
Tunbridge Wells, TN2 5QY
www.spavalleyrailway.co.uk
Tel: 01892 537715

Strathspey Railway
Aviemore, PH22 1PY
www.strathspeyrailway.co.uk
Tel: 01479 810725

Swanage Railway
Swanage, BH19 1HB
www.swanagerailway.co.uk
Tel: 01929 425800

Swindon & Crickslade Steam
Railways
Blunsdon, Wilts.
www.swindon-crickslade-
railway.org.uk
Tel: 01793 771615

Tanfield Railways
Gateshead, NE16 5ET
www.tanfield-railway.co.uk
Tel: 0845 463 4938

Telford Steam Railway
Horsehay, TF4 2NG
www.telfordsteamrailway.
co.uk

Tyseley Railway Centre
670 Warwick Road, Tyseley,
B11 2HL
www.tyseleylocoworks.co.uk
Tel: 01217 084960

West Somerset Railway
Minehead Station, TA24 5BG
Williton Station, TA4 4RQ
Bishops Lydeard, TA4 3RU
www.westsomersetrailway.
co.uk
Tel: 01643 704996